The Spokes of
Venus

The Spokes of Venus

Rebecca Morgan Frank

Carnegie Mellon University Press
Pittsburgh 2016

Acknowledgments

Grateful acknowledgment is made to the following publications in which some of these poems first appeared:

32 Poems: "The Art of Reading," "Conversations with the Artist," "Everybody's a Picasso"; *Crab Orchard Review*: "How to Look at Pictures"; *Hearth*: "Elsewhere"; *International Poetry Review*: "He Was a Good Man"; *Literary Imagination*: "The Way to Sketch"; *The Missouri Review Online*: "The Spokes of Venus"; *Pank*: "Installation in City: Intersections of Bodies"; *New England Review*: "Caught" and "Ministry of Ostriches"; *Ploughshares*: "What Is Left Here"; *Reunion: The Dallas Review*: "How to Build a Rocket"; *Smartish Pace*: "Women, Bird and Stars"; *Southern Humanities Review*: "Bloom"; *The Book of Scented Things: An Anthology of Contemporary Poems Written About or Engaging with Perfumes*: "The Perfumier on the Comeback of the Scented Glove"; *Valley Voices*: "The Morning of the Poem" and "Derby Days"

This book would not exist without the support of the Virginia Center for Creative Arts (VCCA), where much of it was written. Thanks to all of the artists, composers, and writers who have influenced these poems through their own work or their friendship, including the artists who I taught in MassArt's low-residency MFA program at the Fine Arts Work Center in Provincetown, as well as the fellows who I shared time with at VCCA. (A special thanks to Don Joint for his support and to composer Aaron Stepp, who makes collaborating a joy.) Thanks to historian Allison Abra, whose research led me to "Knees Up, Mother Brown!" And special thanks to the following: Phoebe Reeves, for our weekly poem exchanges. My 2013 pop-up writing group of wonderful poets—Rachel Richardson, Kara Candito, Anna Journey, Penelope Pelizzon, and Jennifer Chang. Poets Hadara Bar-Nadav, Andrea Cohen, Gail Mazur, David Barber, Don Bogen, and Angela Ball for their continued guidance and support. The University of Southern Mississippi for its support through research grants and awards. And endless gratitude goes out to my lovely, generous, and ever-expanding community of fellow writers. Finally, a special thanks to my sister, my parents, and John Warrick.

Book design: Connie Amoroso

Library of Congress Control Number 2015945711
ISBN 978-0-88748-606-7

10 9 8 7 6 5 4 3 2

for John

Contents

The Art of Reading

Candlepin, lynchpin, safety pin become
death by fire, hanging, stabbing. Cocktail
becomes the plumage of a male bird
staring me down in the dirt. Napkin
is a sleeping cousin drooling on my bed:
it's noon. Heaven-sent, you smell like
the gods. A word can sock you with a kick,
mock you in a turtleneck, hiding its intent.
Barely. Comedy is two-faced, watching.
Come on, give it a try. Hot dog? Wild
flower? Everything is sweaty and dancing
when you bring back the inanimate.
Looking into its violent core, dormant
but burning to be read right, read wrong.

I.

The Spokes of Venus

Percival Lowell was not the first man to see himself
        in Venus, to see his own shadows on her form, for
                what is love but
a mirror? Yet to see
            oneself so closely
in the atmosphere, the planets as familiar
        as the orb you see them from, this is as the mineral-
           wrought tears of the old stone.

Condensation pearls over porcelain, plaster leaks—
        Something isn't right.
Lowell swore to his own testimony; you see, he'd seen it
        with his own eyes.
                Everything before us
looks like life. The figures we make
           cry because we make them.
The sky is watching us like an eye.

What Is Left Here

Out in the open, there is a cowshed.
There are the expected gaps and hornets.

There lives our story, where we used to meet—
you smelled like hay, were always listening

to some other sound, the buzzing of your own
ideas chasing us down. You began building

a staircase out of thorny branches, then a vest
out of found nests. An angel emerged

from bones and wrenches; a vulture out of junkyard
parts flew in the rafters. Soon the shed was full

of your configurations. You made me pose,
sculpted a rusted wire shadow of me. Sometimes

I saw you watching her while kissing me.
I knew: who wouldn't want to love a mind

like that? I knew: I was part of something.
Now I catalog your works, care for minutiae

of preservation, communications. Loving you
is never over. You knew you made me.

Shaped me here, under gap-leaked light.
Amidst all the other figures of your making.

Caught

after Abraham Walkowitz's *Isadora Duncan*

The artist's hands made her 5,000 times.
They moved as fast as her feet, released
the kinetic into the falling pulse-beat of charcoal

on paper, caught falls poised over surfaces.
His fingers grasped at her movements, wrote,
Her body was music. It was a body electric.

Even her stillness pulsed, crackled on the page:
hands raised overhead, as if asking to be freed
from the very body she made earthly with motion,

her throat lifted for sacrifice, hovering
from a heavenward gaze. Her heartbeat
and breath returned in his drawn timelines.

Notes, words, lines: all that captures her dynamic
renderings are these still shots of the beat
of a bird's wings. He tried to capture flight, motion

in still lifes. The trembling body suspended
with watercolor stains, waiting to be released
from the confines of time. Caught in line.

The Way to Sketch

after Vernon Blake

It is necessary to speak of the rough-
and-ready means. Put aside gamboge
and ochre, rose madder, and aureolin.
Start simple, with the ash and contrast
of two. Everywhere your mind goes,
a line will follow and become a potted
plant, a window view, the beloved's face
warped with your inexperience. Egyptians
held with a supine hand, Greeks,
a closed fist, the modern Chinese strictly
vertical. Position is only one aspect:
beware of the confidence and hesitancy
of youth. A pause can become stillness, where
nothing comes to life. Too bold, you can't
undo your heavy clasp and mark. Yes,
there is terror in becoming the creator.
Recall the kewpie as it stepped off the page
and built itself in bisque, celluloid, then plastic—
grinning from its plump-made ways.
Stay horizontal on the page. Best
to stick with a kneadable eraser,
pliable to any shape. Takes care of mistakes.

The Perfumier on the Comeback of the Scented Glove

I.
Artifice is easy: the palms leathered
with perfume are no mirror for
the gardener's hands, but mimic each
flower, bush, and tree tended.
For there is no work in beauty, as
natural as a lemon grove, an early
blossom, the greengage plum.

II.
At its start, perfume was a verb,
by its end, a noun.
As is hand what we have
and what we give. The glove
is a popular gift.

III.
They can be worn, can
cover your lover's hands so when
touching the other, she blossoms
in pear, grapefruit, pruneau, bergamot—
the scent designed for you.
You would come between them
wherever they went.

IV.
If not the hand, then around
the throat, silver
pomander opening
like the wedges of an orange,
fending off the body's odors

with sandalwood, cedar
masking the cloying of decay.
Every fad has its own end.
Everything returns.

Conversations with the Artist (1)

I've always felt as if I were in a cage.
If I stick out an arm, I'm seen as wanting
and taking. A leg: my violence is noted.
When I mentioned the suffocation by
my father, they made it autobiographical.
The subtext of my work in iron has been
ignored, lost in discussions of time, not space.
What you'll never understand about
installations is that everyone else is always
outside of them. I'm stuck inside. The move
toward deliberate transience is the mark of a fool.
If disappearing is inevitable, you must fight it.
No one misses the prisoner.
The bars are like a frame: you want in
as much as I have always wanted out.

Ministry of Ostriches

It's hard to tell if all the tresses are taken
from horse, human, sheep, bird, yak

or buffalo. The part like an even hem,
stitched. All dyed an apricot shade,

a golden hue, bleached white, stained
night-black with an edge of Persian blue.

A cake of scented wax was once thought
to cool you as it melted over the surface

of your hot hat of hair. The risk? A blessing
could stick to the fibers and leave you

more a sinner than when you had shorn
your scalp bare in adulterous affairs.

It's not just that vanity is a cultural play:
at heart a wig holds in its build the act

of sacrifice—all that hair removed at cost
to be what someone else's fingers ran through.

There must have been a queen somewhere who
shaved her rival's head and wore the curls in

triumph. She quickly learned that wearing
other peoples' blessings was a curse.

To wear another's love is to be a wolf
dressed as a lamb to slaughter. Surely

everyone knows a horse or a child will yank
off your airs and see you as bare and fuzzy

as an ostrich, mouth open, declaring it
has got nothing to hide in open court.

Sogetto Cavato

Lovers are hidden everywhere around us.
Listen—their vowels are carved out and buried
in the symphony itself. I could translate you
into tones, hide you in the *cantus firmus*
where you'd remain untouched, unseen.
No one would even suspect you're in there
as the counterpoint to butterflies gorging
on the bush, the fogged blue skyline brightening,
all of the tropes of nature I'd hide you in.
You'd never recognize your name's throaty
vowels made notes. Perhaps my love
is for the scholar of a hundred years hence
who hears my longing's notes, who finds my
loving signature of you. He'll learn to love
me back for how I dissolved you in; he'll
love me for my cleverness: our secret. It's fine.
Love is at a distance at its best.

Conversations with the Artist (2)

My first teacher told me
     that what sculpture involved
was being a God. He was not talking

about the old ways, about fashioning
     a man out of a rib.
Out of the earth. A god can see something

that does not exist yet in the world. Who
     could have imagined the giraffe,
the octopus, the flounder? Who

could have imagined our sharp sensibilities,
     our contortions? The materials
are all there—eyes and blood and respiration,

but still, they get made new. Now I know
     that these days such a view
is against science, but the idea of a god is as real

as god is not. A scientist who sees
     what has been done
versus one who can make straw out of gold.

Or more like plastic out of petroleum.
     Paper out of trees. You
have to decide which kind you will be.

We're mistaken when we equate the wise
     and the prophetic. You're always
looking either backwards or forwards.

This piece puts you on a precipice.
        It's up to you
which way you fall. You see—it's all there.

The scientist and the artist were once one—
        how else could you record
what you saw? How else, find a way of seeing?

How to Judge a Picture

Everyone in the room is cheering.
This is what you do for a painting you love!
We climb up on one another's shoulders,
wave pom-poms that match the palette.
We want to buy the season tickets to the train
that huffs through this landscape. We want
to climb the towers of this steely sculpture
and hang the flag. Victory is ours! We have
seen something to love here. Outside the gallery,
there is an alley full of garbage. Beauty stops
at the door. A scraggly tree is coming out
of the pavement where the people are lined
up, cigarettes and cell phones, waiting
for a chance to look. They keep their
giant fingers in their bags. Wear T-shirts
of their favorite teams of artist assistants.
On the alley wall, someone has drawn
a hillside and a horse. A young man sits
on a crate and peels the glue from under
his nails. He nods. And looks. And soon,
pulls out the chalk and adds a saddle
and a man, who looks back and shouts
as if he has found his enemy again.

"Landscape is my Pleasure"

after Thomas Gainsborough's *Coastal Scene with Shipping and Cattle*

Even a cow can enjoy the view,
look out at the sails in longing.
In search of greener pastures,

of course, but who wouldn't be—
feeling the hard rock beneath,
forced to the precipice by all

the same old crowd of family
and friends. And yes, even
a cow has enemies, thinks

he'd like to ship one off to
sea. Why can't they just join
the marines? Or study painting

in Italy? Who says a cow can't
have dreams? Below, these humans
bear just as much chance

of escape as the beasts. After lunch
they'll go back to herding, leave
views' visions until the work is done.

On the Symbolism of the Lamb

title after Hermann Nitsch

The artist rips the small body open, reaches his hand
into the bowels of the lamb after tearing its toughly
tender skin, previously shaved. Recalls the Dionysian
ritual. He calls it action. Art now flesh. The lamb is pink
and blue. *Little Lamb, Little Lamb*—Allen Ginsberg sings.
Sings, *He is meek and mild, / he became a child.* Abraham's knife
throats his lamb of a son, ready to lay his guts on the altar
for a god. Sings Blake, *Little Lamb who made thee?* The artist
carefully places the entrails on the table. His son will become
a shepherd of a Soho artist. A purist. Sharpens his own
knife. Sings, *Why does the lamb love [Abraham] so?* First,
he will only eat meat, then he will never eat meat, then
he will only eat what he has carved with his buck knife.
He visits the gallery a captured coyote circled for three days,
leaving the heart of the artist in the room untouched.
I Like America and America Likes Me, the artist says. My father
once held the knife, Isaac says. Now every time I eat lamb,
I imagine it's my own flesh. Self-cannibalizing, that's where it's at.
Lights. Cameras. Watch me, *little lamb.* Everyone's watching. This
takes sacrifice. Faith. The galleries are packed. I'll take an arm,
a leg. I'm not afraid. I'll chew the gristle of my own heart.

Bloom

after Anna Shuleit's installation *Bloom* at the
Massachusetts Mental Health Center

I saw the hint of something godlike, removed
from the mineral and green of the yard

outside the chapel. The hospital's peeling
halls packed with blossoms, as if

mold had become seed and everything rancid,
fetid, bloomed. I walked into your old

room. A rusted frame, the windowpane
jagged beneath the bolted bars. A sky

outside would have been yours before
they tore out your eyes. That's what you said,

their lightning blazed your body and made
the world go dark. The edges dull and then

the pills drowned out the sound and then, then,
you said, you repeated again and again,

then, they took my legs, my arms, my
mouth, the tongue a rag that absorbed

no taste. A life of wasting muscle and
teeth turned black from the sugary contra-

band your father smuggled in his pockets,
doubled by the way you filled your cup

with more sugar than tea. You showed me
pictures of the day they set you free. You

had killed a man, served the rest of your
childhood. Four months later, had me.

Your burial was early, my freedom
late. I fingered the bars, the wet glass

tear, and imagined your escape. We
were condemned: the building, your body

and mine that came of you and some
other part. Silence, seeping through.

Women, Bird and Stars

after Miro

I'm made of steel cord, which appears
delicate from a distance, as does telephone

wire shivering under the stars and sun.
A bird comes to rest on me and neither

of us has a song for this. I'm afraid
to confess that bird bones feel heavy.

Still, I can feel the hollowness and want
to stuff it with threads and lint and glitter:

all the things I hate. It wants to feed me
worms, watch me squirm. I pucker up

and flap, the galaxies are hard to access
from here, where everything is flat.

I hop like a bird; the bird snickers
and flies off. I can't, I won't—

I try to jump up, be light, but he
has drawn in my hips too heavy.

Figure Drawing

The only time I knew an artist's naked
model, she was vain. Posing takes
a certain stance, requires a vacant
glaze; before long the adjacent
artists all become complacent
when faced daily with a beauty
so self-fabricated, a labored duty.

I always wondered what she craved,
how her brittle bones and birthmarks,
her sunken stomach, felt the gaze.
Frankly, in her own work, she was brazen.
It wasn't that she simply desired praise:
she got that. Perhaps it was her need
to be made into something, a greed

to fill not just her own art (of words),
but theirs. Who doesn't want a cameo,
but what if hundreds of those were secured?
And as the artists grew younger, you matured?
What if the world becomes inured
to your angled grace held captive?
A risk, to need to be made in form to live.

Everybody's a Picasso

The tongue can be recreated, as can the cheek,
the scalp, the nose. Parts of the body relocated
to necessary service, rendering the doctors all
into Picassos. I've had my eye transferred
to my chin so I can read the fine print. My foot
moved next to my ear so I can hear myself walking
home at night. My lips are now on my forehead
so you don't have to slouch when you kiss me goodbye.
Every new configuration makes the world look twice,
but I am the queen of efficiency. I came out
like a two-headed cat with one of the heads missing.
I have been looking at it ever since. I am waiting
for the kind of love that comes in a transformer kit,
wielded by one who will put all my parts back
where they belong. One who listens to my own
footsteps for me. Who lends me his eyes.

Magic with Cards

Oh! This is the hallmark of celestial
tricks: the magician lifts his hat
and says, Look at this! So much pointing
we've forgotten what we're looking
at. The rabbit even looks confused
and orders a double latte. No, he turns
into a scarf. I'm trying to write the script
but every show throws me for a loop.
Audience participation means someone
can scream, or choke on a coin that ends
in her throat rather than behind her ear.
While on the stage, a man carved in two
wobbles his torso over to tie a loose shoelace.
I shuffle the deck and ask you to please pick
a card. Spades, I'll walk away. Hearts, you
can play your next trick on me. But that's it.

Knees Up, Mother Brown!

after the 1939 popular song and dance

Each body part implies a different command.
Surrender (of hands, feet, bottom) turns to pride—
a lifted chin and the joy of the knee knocking
up up up: "Knees Up, Mother Brown!" The mad
nest of dancers clocks one another in the legs
and arms and chest and the song itself says
it best—*oh what a rotten song, oh what a . . . knees
up Mother*—who? Kick in the jiggle of hip, and slip
your hands around your partner's waist. There
was a time when you could slip out for a quick
dance on the break. Sure was better than a shot
or a smoke, a box of doughnuts, a toke: Let's bring it
back. Clap! Lift up those knees. Please? *Mrs. Brown
you've got a lovely*—no? Different song? Lift
your knees and think of England. We're dancing
mad. There's nothing like the sin of it, mid-day.
Let's make a comeback for the Queen and let's
begin right above the knees, at the hem. Everyone
is looking around for something to go crazy about, again.

What Every Pianist Needs to Know about the Body

title after Thomas Mark

Dear Pianist, I have been reading that Disembodiment
is a disaster and that you are at risk. I would ask you

to please hold on to your body. I have been reading that
there are bones that make the music: I should not imagine

that you feel your way across the keys. Skin is a body's
passive part. Apparently I should not just be worried

about your finger bones but also about your skull
and your vertebrae and all of the other attachments

to the arms I watch in concert. Pianist, you already know
all of this. But to me, as the ears you depend on are part of me,

at first, I was not thinking about you. Did you know
there are bones in the ear? My dear, dear pianist, you assume

that your movements produce sound. When I move,
I hear string quartets in my head. When you move,

I barely hear. The doctor says it won't be long until
I can only see your body move. Sometimes it happens now.

It is beautiful.
What everyone else hears is just the side effect.

Elsewhere

He is nowhere to be found. She has looked
in the basement, in the eaves of the attic,
in the studio where the parts of everything
pile like a misplaced junkyard. He is everywhere,
in the glasses shelved too high in the kitchen,
the unsharpened pencils on the old phone table.
He is in the still forms, the collaged masks lining
the hallway, eyelessly staring at her. He settles
in the cracks of her thoughts as she tries
to write. Even elsewhere, she is in his shadow.
The museum calls. The gallery calls. If she turns
off the phone, is that turning her back? She can see
his face pleading in each doorway. Brushing its teeth
in the bathroom mirror. He's hungry for breakfast.
He'd eat it at every meal if he could. She begins
to understand traditions where they leave out
food for the dead. She considers an exorcism,
but wonders what would be left. The metaphor
for love she's looking at include parasite, cannibal,
the clouds. Everywhere, she writes. Elsewhere.

On Making

I held a jackhammer once.
It matched me

in height and weight and I
planned destruction, ripped

everything solid from the ground.
The concrete was my prey,

but it was the tool I fought
to master, its metal body

trembling beneath my hands.
Or, perhaps, its electric heart

was what shook me through
my last held bones.

The concrete, gone,
the rented machinery, returned—

and I wondered if Sisyphus had imagined
a garden where the rock came from.

II.

How to Look at Pictures

title after Robert Clermont Witt, 1906

Refuse to make eye contact with the subject.
He has been following you around the gallery.
You are certain that he can see down your shirt.
Look at other subjects, but know that they, too,
are not of primary interest. Even when they watch
you. Try not to consider what happened
to the small girl staring furiously, the thin-faced
woman wanly looking away. Do not think about
what they had for breakfast, if the bread was hard.
Certainly do not consider the odors underneath
their arms and skirts. Do not allow a breeze into
the room they sit in. Do not assume I am talking
about any painting: step away from the subject.
All subject. Was the painter in love? Do not ask
the question. Imagine you are the painter,
blocking out everything you don't want to see.
Everything is out of the picture. Stop looking.
Stop seeking what isn't there. Tuck your narratives
back in your pocket. Look for perspective, light,
shade. Let your eyes wander back to the girl.
She is trying to say something but her mouth
has been painted deliberately shut. Her lips, thin.

After

after Don Joint's "Abstraction after Uccello's *Battle of San Romano*"

Pigment changes the past's ass
into a *coeur*. The graphic remains.
The gradual loss of the surface
accelerates with one hand on
the switch. It's an aerial view,
the voyeur's switch and bait.
Look away and the colors have
faded blood, buried the love
of death in the frame. Still,
stained, the action builds
behind the caution. Narrative
stays primary into the long view.
Make no mistake, the voyeur
turning heads, the naked body
it takes, continues to be you.

The Chief of Staff

after an Akan Linguist Staff, 19th–20th century

No one can touch the ceremonial staff except
the leader's advisor. For even from here these
ears that line the scepter look solid gold.
Everyone believes the leader hears everything,
fears nothing. (His ears, as the proverb says,
are as big as those of an elephant.) But beneath
the intricate gold leaf is wood, porous,
and the sounds make their way through the long
body, begin the rot of doubt. The chief's
linguist feels the staff grow lighter, now
a symbol of how a leader, left long untouched
in his council's circle, never hears anything.
The people, meanwhile, are speaking in tongues,
making their own gold code. Breaking the rod.

Morpheus, from the Wall

He always finds me bolt upright, eyes painted wide,
or bent over my desk, weary of the figures before me.

Soporific son of other gods—I like his sleepy glance and I—
shameless narcoleptic falling down his stare—

[Hypnotist, he is everywhere]
I comply.

Why stay awake and toil and tussle towards
nothing more than his arms anyway?

But when this shifty god of sleep, some soft peace,
tries to seal my lids against the clock I watch

in wait for my lover's late return—
Beware young god: my chastity is saved.

Objects Are Softer Than They Appear

I have bitten into Claes Oldenberg's *Good Humor*.
It's a little Neopolitan, dressed in animal print,
perched on wooden staffs and furry on the tongue.
You are pretending to fall into a pile of old teddy bears.
Art has become plush, even the couch in the center
of the gallery has no organs of steel or wood:
there's a blow-up doll of a living room, reminiscent
of the Barbie dream house we blew into three
dimensions. There's a padded gallery to bang
our heads, full of yarned instruments
we're all meant to play on. "It's the critic's job,"
you suck your lip and say, "to undo the stitches.
Release the seams, let out the air with a knife.
Right?" I shrug, keep looking. Bite.

The Morning of the Poem

after James Schuyler and Anna Shuleit

She is painting portraits from the ground up, is still
        on feet, bare or in heels, or now a foot
that wears a white sock yet still has naked toes.

Lately she has made it to calves, even knees, sits
        in cafés and sketches strangers, peers under
tables for gestures turned in hesitation, reaching.

Captures acts of bicycling, stepping, unsure
        when she'll travel further up the body. Not once
do I look at her bare legs, her hands a swarm of bees.

She says she no longer feels obliged to fill full
        spaces, no longer feels slave to shape
and size of canvas, and I think about space, all

the untouched surface I've abandoned, imagine making
        marks on poem after poem in a row. Today's mark,
pulled blindly from the library shelf's *The Art of Skating,*

is *the unemployed lower limb.* Across the aisle Julian Schnabel
        paints Duende and Zeus in blue, the latter shrinking
and I read *the employed knee is bent.* I look under

the table wondering if my knees are employed or unemployed:
        they uncross, switch views and still, I'm unsure, while
in the photo a man arabesques across the ice, and the red

paint reads like blood as if the God and the Duende
        underneath can only be a violent smear across the page,
and in my the next poem, *The Art of Skating* evokes

a short skirt, legs wrapped around one another like a swivel
       cone, arms mirroring overhead—the poem is spinning
and whirls right to the third poem where the skater is lifted

above a man's head: this poem is a duet, and then I'm thinking
       about Anna's new painting the one with the wider canvas
where there are now two sets of legs but space in between.

If falling out of love calls for white space, then the first poem,
       the poem of the morning of the poem, the initial canvas,
is in love. My legs seek employment, work their way up

to the wooden chair, cross themselves underneath
       me. If the painter goes looking she won't find them
anywhere—she'll think they've walked right off of her canvas, looking
       for a new canvas to step into and employ themselves.

Abstracts

after Franz Kline's *Cardinal*

Ship's anchor bows to the refuse at the peak
of the winding blacktop of lines.

The body's upstroke ends like a quill.
And still, the hoop is abandoned at the bottom of the well.

This is the cardinal sin hopping over the barbed wire
to reach the white, leaving the octopus spray.

The wisp belayed down beneath the foreground
lies: there was a whale, a wile, a wandering

nod to the language's quickest tic,
marked with no translation.

You see what you mean and he vanishes turpentine,
turpentine: it's all design of darkness. Appalled.

Gallery Night

Steel girders frame the sky tonight—we raise
our billowing arms like tents and beckon
everyone in. The outsiders are their own
installation behind the glass of the building.
They stare in, pass by. Frown in confusion.
Light overflows the corners and floods faces
white, like a kabuki theatre of patrons
playing out small talk and wonder. The truth
is that there's nothing in the room but us.
We are the made, we are the eyes. Later
I wonder if it doesn't prove why the past
threw in a horse, a dog, a part of portrait
that makes us all seem more human.

The Artist at the Residency

He compiled a series of objects
and set them on the table:
a gold pendant with a large
Burmese ruby, a fresh-plucked
Narcissus, a flute. These were
arranged. And dismissed.
Then china and peaches
were commandeered.
Shadows were made, erased.
When the clock struck lunch,
he removed them all and gathered
a series of bodies to drape
over the couches and cloths.
By dinner they, too, were
gone. An easel was taken
to the lakeside. Left there for
someone to gather. Supplies
were sent for. Meals delivered.
A cellist was summoned
to play outside the studio windows.
The horses were removed
from the pasture view, then
replaced with darker ones.
The train was rerouted for silence.
He was taken to the cemetery
and then the battlefield. He was
left alone for days. He was allowed
to smoke in his studio. Bourbon
bottles were replaced outside his door.
When he left, they found the sheets
untouched. The canvases unstretched.

Conversations with the Artist (3)

Snake venom is supposed to cure snakebites—
it is simply a matter of swallowing
what is already in your blood, even if
it has been dormant for years, that infected hurt.
You were a child once; you bit. You were ruthless
in a way the hated child is—the parents want to say
to one another, he's a bad apple. But they can't.
They have to treat the venom like love and love
it back. Watch it grow like disease. Weren't we talking
about me, about my work? I use my blood
because it has been poisoned. Because it is sweet
to the taste when I lick my fingers, congeals
on the surface like damage. I never hurt anyone
when I was a child, but the bees found me, stung my
hands until they swelled up like mitts. The dog pushed me
out of my bed. I knew what it was to be a victim. I screamed
all night and they sent her to live on a farm. It wasn't
a euphemism. You see, my fear was what freed her.
That's what I hope for my art. I want to free you. Free
the rotten apple. Free the domestics we
have all become. Blood is pure. The only medium.

How to Build a Rocket

Feel it first. No
there's got to be
a base, a stop-
watch top, a big
point to it all
on top. Wait. Stop.
Crop the jets. Set
aside more glue.
Send it to your
ceiling, watch it
doesn't get caught
in the fan. No,
wait. Go back. First
make a moon out
of marbles for
it to dream of.
Plant seeds in each
murky glass hill.
Let it glow, lob
it up past some
distant planet. No,
wait. It needs
its own rocket to
even leave our earth.
Which came first, this
rocket or that
moon? Come on,
it was the rocket
maker, the one
who sketched the moons
for this. For us.

There's No Ornament Like a Menagerie

You've been collecting them like a Prince.
There was the giraffe at the 42nd Street stop,
the elephant on the escalator at Macy's. Six
armadillos in a bar downtown. A tiger who
was sitting in a café on the Upper East Side.
They're easy to lure. Old magazines, chewing
gum, a ride on your tandem bike. Sometimes
everyone's in need of a change. You can coach it
like a vacation, a spa where you never work
another day in your life. Regular meal service.
Housekeeping. Once the peacock comments
about getting by on his looks. The lion
grumbles about the regular workouts. But
it's the monkey who says, smacking her gum,
that she misses industry, labor, clocking in.
You shrug. Swing for some new landscaping.
Your child is the one who actually runs away, leaves
a note: I'm tired of looking, seeing, watching,
witnessing, noticing, peering, and all that.
I want to get noticed. Find an agent, a show
of my own. Maybe the big screen, maybe Vegas.
It's time to set out on my own, to stop looking.

Derby Days

The horses are sleeping and the paintings
are awake. The horses in the paintings are
watching the people who are awake waiting
for the horses to wake up and run. The man
who painted the horses is awake somewhere
else painting something else: a swan, a
Doberman staring at an apple. Someone
shoots an arrow at the apple and the core splits.
This is all in the painting that is not
in the gallery where the people are watching
here in the new city. What the new city
and the old have in common are people watching.
The women wear hats. The men place bets
as a way to interact with the art of shank
and shudder and full speed ahead. *Feels like
Derby Week*, a man says. Everybody nods.
Keeps watching. Takes a sip. Down in the gallery,
the horse in the painting closes his eyes and dreams
of racing, of leaving stills and pulling ahead.
Of someday winning the art of the track.

Retrospective

Once there was a man who whittled,
then another who built. Finally, a guy
who chopped down trees in patterns,
made a forest into a work of art.

The throats of saplings were sliced
and served as bouquets on banquet
tables. They sang *hey, dolly, dolly, hey
nonny hey,* they sang *boil boil toil*

and trouble, they sang, *it's gonna take
a lotta love* and the trees held hands
and held vigil and the audience picked
their teeth with shards of tree and

the photographs captured everything
from above as if someone was surveilling
because you see you can't get away from
censorship: they are fundraising to buy

trees to fill in the gaps, to erase the art—
it was never a commentary on nations,
but on population, she explained.

"He Was a Good Man"

The roosters are blooming and dying
and she is but a hen, her cluck, stuck
in soprano tune-out, the lockout
of the lady, the ma'am—the one
who understands is hemming up her
sleeve. What we hear is not
a good thing ever came from someone
good, no art, no lasting line to recite—
the woman with wit, perhaps,
has the laugh last, for when the flip
of dirt ensures your death, you can lay to rest
She was a good woman. No, it won't do.
She was a good man: that, however,
she would have lived through. Being
good at something that lets you be good
at instead of good. Bless her, it's true.
She was a better man (read: artist) than you.

Notes for the Eye (of Head of a Woman)

The eyeball isn't pretty at all. Veiny, cloudy, might bounce.

Stone emptied the eye, left surface to the imagination.

The eye miniature presumes that only a lover will recognize such a portrait.

The art of eye making began with clay.

Miro's woman looks like a mutant alien glancing back toward home.

The thick view of the Romans and Egyptians later turned to glass by the Venetians.

If your right eye causes you to sin, tear it out and throw it away.

Now a giant eyeball tours the States. You can see it anywhere.

Remember that even animals have eyes. (95%.)

An astronaut's eye is flatter each time he returns from space.

Capturing how an eye sees rather than how it has been seen.

The retina is similar to film.

Gaze, gauche, (consider the veil as a frame?), gelatinous.

Start with the hand, end with the eye.

Refract, detect, depth, field—the space around the eye expands.

The Artist's Ode to And Per Se And

Amp up your and, give it a hand toward a pretty little
makeover, a bit more swerve and curl: give it sump gumption.

Purse your lips and say something, anything equivalent.
Inside it and beside it and on top of it, additionally.

It's the type that holds hands, commands—and
reprimands. A sign for a sign, it brings things together

as it translates itself. Accumulation its strong point
directed to more and to the end in its own equivalence.

O, and per se and, you always know where to land,
as you remand us to where we once began. But

to tell you the truth, you're meaningless, and bland.
Even in this shapely little suit, you're no more than well cut.

The Most Commonly Asked Question
about the Glass Flowers

These stems have met their maker, the steady tool
their union. Each color drafted to the honest pink
of a life. He watched the original wilt before
his eyes as he shaped its dark nicks, its flaws.
His unyielding frigid petals have no scent.
Are they really glass? Despite the signs, I ask.
The mind's eye deceives the yes, trapped
between the life I see and the cold hard glass
reality I'm not allowed to touch. My senses
fail me. I want to pinch their delicate ruse,
prove it real. Watch them shrivel. The facts:
No breath, never has been. Except the one above
their lie. In here, the hand is the flower.

The Piece Need Not Be Built

title after Lawrence Weiner

Bodies are moving across my mind: they mark
the music in the elevator, the store, the concert hall.

I look around, afraid others can see
all this movement. I twitch and pulse: my body

wants to be the bodies in my mind.
Perhaps they will restrain me, tighten the white

bands. They'll turn the music off. But still,
I'll hear it, replay the familiar chords in my head

and make the bodies move. Then, I am
a god. (Why must I keep still?) I must

make my mind actualize on other bodies,
on stages, bare itself in front of a series

of still bodies. They can anticipate the chords
but not what I'll have done to them. All

forms of notation are useless—perhaps the piece
must be built, but it never will be. The materials

are other Bodies and here I am, bound,
and waiting. The medicine keeps me from even

pointing my toes. But still I move—beneath
the surface. Still, I make and arch and sing

with every muscle but my throat and lungs.
My mind, the movement. The music mine.

Installation by Sea: Body Navigations

Archipelago of bodies bending in sheared white fog. A solitary
thigh, bunched and quivering, extends. Throats
curve up to sky; night's pass is blood knifed on rock.
Bodies move, a migration along the shoreline.
Like lovers, like flocks, flinging and contracting, sea
salting their eyes, they spread along the heights, and bodies
bound off the cliff, arched in grace, one by one, circling in the foam,
a gasping rise, as an aria of arms opens the light, the sun breaks
and burns them off the surfaces.
        A dancer left, lone, on the pebbled
shore, opens her mouth and sings. It's a terrible keen, the clutch
of a soundless throat. Her body won't move. Her voice floats.

Installation in City: Intersections of Bodies

Gray knots of limbs, legs wrapped through crooks,
a chain link gang of bodies boring its way through
the street. No weight supports its own. The hands
walk concrete, knees scrape, a head hovers over
the curb: traffic bends and boldens around it, not
stopped but startled out of symmetry. Hands wave
from the mass of bodies, the bulk of automobiles,
and then the beast unfurls, flings
                    a fragile frame out in leaps of grass,
a round ass to the grate shadowed by a truck, three
tall men in tights unravel, unrolling up to the skyscraper roofs,
lost in sight to the endless supply of tiny bodies spinning
out, out into the gaps between the cars, dervishes
unwrapping capes like wings and the intersection flies—
the cars kill their engines. The city stops.

Installation in Interior: Café Mélange

They roll from underneath the tables. Crawl out
from the bar, climb down ropes from the chandeliers.
An army of shiny pink and yellow bodies slither,
drape themselves across the tables, fingers
dripping into dinner plates, wine spilling across
their chests like exploded hearts. They grab startled
diners by their portly waists and whittle them with spins.
The chef's pas de deux with the maître d' begins
with an embrace over the cart of cakes. A waltz
married to a techno beat gets the last patrons
off their feet and toward the door. *Mais non!*—
the dancers disappear through hidden doors
in the floor, a new round of platters appears at each
place. Stained, the diners return to their seats
and gorge, the glowing dancers' bodies glued outside on
windows, crawling up, like moths on a screen. *Scene.*

Nephelokokkugia

I, too, have sought out the company of birds,
the league between men and gods.
A city of twine and glittering lost ribbons
and beads binding the twigs and leaves.

As above, so below—but here lies
a liminal, virginal island of clouds.
Reachable and far from the preaches
and smacks, the theological tactics.

And from here, a view: see the curtains
open and close below you while the gods'
footsteps still shake your ceiling. But you
know it's only thunder, and the vista

just a reflection in the glinting seas.
And that quarrels have wings, transmogrify,
their foul breath steady from body to body,
their raspy insistence spanning elevations.

For there's only one land, this cloudy
one of cuckoos shot, gutted and stuffed,
turned parrots of the same rhetoric
of the apish and the robed.

So now dream not of clouds but of some
inner power to act as your muse.
Kneel at the foot of the glare. Close your eyes:
it's best not to look into the nuclear burn.